Joseph and the Coat of Many Colors

Genesis 37:3-36, 39:1-45:15

Retold by Pamela Broughton
Illustrated by Pamela Ford Johnson

A GOLDEN BOOK® • NEW YORK

Jacob was an old man who had twelve sons. He lived with them in the land called Canaan.

Jacob loved one son, Joseph, best of all. He gave Joseph a coat of many colors, to show his love.

That made Joseph's brothers jealous.

A short time later, Joseph had two dreams. In the first dream, he and his brothers were tying bundles of grain in a field. Joseph's bundle rose up, and his brothers' bundles bowed down before it.

In the second dream, the sun, the moon, and eleven stars bowed down before Joseph.

Joseph told his brothers and his father about the dreams. His father said, "Shall I and your mother and brothers bow down before you?"

Then Joseph's brothers grew more jealous.

   One day, when the brothers were caring for their
sheep in the fields, Jacob sent Joseph to bring back
news of them.
   When the brothers saw Joseph coming, they decided
to kill him.

But the oldest brother, Reuben, said, "Let's throw Joseph into a pit, but let's not kill him," for Reuben meant to rescue Joseph.

When Joseph reached the place, his brothers took his many-colored coat. They threw Joseph into a deep hole.

Soon a camel caravan passed on its way to Egypt.
Reuben was away. His brother Judah suggested that
they sell Joseph to the caravan traders, to be a slave.
All the brothers agreed.

After they had sold Joseph, the brothers took his coat
and dipped it in the blood of an animal. Then they
took the coat to their father.

When Jacob saw the coat, he thought Joseph had
been killed by a wild beast. He wept for his lost son,
and refused to be comforted.

But God was with Joseph.

In Egypt, he was sold to Potiphar, the captain of the king's guard. Potiphar liked Joseph, and put him in charge of his household.

Potiphar's wife hated Joseph, and she told lies about him to her husband. So at last, Potiphar had Joseph thrown into prison.

The chief jailer liked Joseph. He put Joseph in charge of all the other prisoners.

One day, the king grew angry with his cupbearer
and his baker. He had them thrown into the prison.

A night came when they each had a dream. The next
morning, they told their dreams to Joseph. Joseph
knew that God would help him understand the dreams.
He was able to tell them what their dreams meant: The
baker was to be killed, but the cupbearer would be
released to serve the king again.

Joseph said to the cupbearer, "Remember me when
it goes well with you, for I have done nothing wrong."

In three days, the baker was hanged and the cupbearer stood before the king again, just as Joseph had said.

But the cupbearer forgot about Joseph.

Two years later, the king had a dream, and no one could tell him what it meant. Then the cupbearer remembered Joseph, who was still in prison. Joseph was brought before the king.

Joseph told the king that his dream meant there would be seven years of plenty in Egypt, followed by seven years of famine.

The king was pleased with Joseph. He put him in charge of the whole kingdom, to build storehouses for the extra food that would grow during the years of plenty.

Just as Joseph had said, the crops grew well for
seven years. Joseph stored the extra grain.

After seven years, there was famine everywhere.
Only in Egypt was there plenty to eat, because of the
grain Joseph had stored.

There was no food in Canaan, where Jacob and his sons lived. So Jacob sent his sons to Egypt to buy food. He did not send Benjamin with them. Benjamin was his youngest son, and Jacob was afraid something might happen to him.

When Jacob's sons came to Egypt, they went to Joseph and bowed before him, just as Joseph's dream had foretold.

Joseph recognized his brothers, but they did not recognize him.

Joseph questioned them about their homeland and their family. Then Joseph said, "You are spies!"

"No," the brothers replied. "We came to buy food."

"If you are honest men," Joseph said, "one of you will remain here while the rest bring food to your family. Then come back with your youngest brother."

One brother remained in Egypt, while the others returned home. When the food was all eaten, Jacob told his sons to return to Egypt and buy more grain. He told them to take Benjamin back with them. "Return to the great ruler in Egypt. And God grant that he may release your brother and send you all safely home."

So they took presents for Joseph, and returned to Egypt.

When Joseph saw his brothers, he ordered his
servants to bring them to his house. The brothers
were surprised when Joseph sat down with them to
eat a meal.

Joseph gave them grain. Then he told his servants to hide a silver cup in Benjamin's sack. The brothers left.

Joseph sent his servants after them, to accuse them of stealing the cup. Joseph wanted to make his brothers come back, so he could tell them who he was. The brothers were brought back to Joseph's house.

Joseph told them then that he was their brother. He told them to return to Canaan and bring all Jacob's family back with them to Egypt, to live in honor and plenty.

"Now you see," he said, "you did not send me here. God sent me, to save you and all my people from hunger."